How To Use This Study Guide

This five-lesson study guide corresponds to *"Partnering With Jesus and Working With God" With Rick Renner* (Renner TV). Each lesson in this study guide covers a topic that is addressed during the program series, with questions and references supplied to draw you deeper into your own private study of the Scriptures on this subject.

To derive the most benefit from this study guide, consider the following:

First, watch or listen to the program prior to working through the corresponding lesson in this guide. (Programs can also be viewed at **renner.org** by clicking on the Media/Archives links or on our Renner Ministries YouTube channel.)

Second, take the time to look up the scriptures included in each lesson. Prayerfully consider their application to your own life.

Third, use a journal or notebook to make note of your answers to each lesson's Study Questions and Practical Application challenges.

Fourth, invest specific time in prayer and in the Word of God to consult with the Holy Spirit. Write down the scriptures or insights He reveals to you.

Finally, take action! Whatever the Lord tells you to do according to His Word, do it.

For added insights on this subject, it is recommended that you obtain Rick Renner's books *Sparkling Gems From the Greek, Volumes 1* and *2*. You may also select from Rick's other available resources by placing your order at **renner.org** or by calling 1-800-742-5593.

LESSON 1

TOPIC

A Decision To Partner With Jesus From the Very Beginning

SCRIPTURES

1. **2 Corinthians 6:1** — We then, as workers together with him…. [We are "co-workers" with God.]
2. **Matthew 2:1-3** — Now when Jesus was born in Bethlehem of Judaea in the days of Herod the king, behold, there came wise men from the east to Jerusalem, Saying, Where is he that is born King of the Jews? for we have seen his star in the east, and are come to worship him. When Herod the king had heard these things, he was troubled, and all Jerusalem with him.
3. **Matthew 2:8-11** — And he [Herod] sent them to Bethlehem, and said, Go and search diligently for the young child; and when ye have found him, bring me word again, that I may come and worship him also. When they had heard the king, they departed; and, lo, the star, which they saw in the east, went before them, till it came and stood over where the young child was. When they saw the star, they rejoiced with exceeding great joy. And when they were come into the house, they saw the young child with Mary his mother, and fell down, and worshipped him: and when they had opened their treasures, they presented unto him gifts; gold, and frankincense, and myrrh.

GREEK WORDS

1. "co-worker" — συνεργός (*sunergos*): compound of σύν (*sun*) and ἔργον (*ergon*); σύν (*sun*) is a preposition that connects one to another, hence, it carries the idea of partnership; the word ἔργον (*ergon*) depicts work or a task; compounded, two or more who are joined together in a common job or task
2. "behold" — ἰδού (*idou*): bewilderment, shock, amazement, and wonder
3. "wise men" — μάγος (*magos*): plural form, magi; group of priests and astronomers and strongly influenced by Daniel; king-makers

A Note From Rick Renner

I am on a personal quest to see a "revival of the Bible" so people can establish their lives on a firm foundation that will stand strong and endure the test as end-time storm winds begin to intensify.

In order to experience a revival of the Bible in your personal life, it is important to take time each day to read, receive, and apply its truths to your life. James tells us that if we will continue in the perfect law of liberty — refusing to be forgetful hearers, but determined to be doers — we will be blessed in our ways. As you watch or listen to the programs in this series and work through this corresponding study guide, I trust you will search the Scriptures and allow the Holy Spirit to help you hear something new from God's Word that applies specifically to your life. I encourage you to be a doer of the Word He reveals to you. Whatever the cost, I assure you — it will be worth it.

> Thy words were found, and I did eat them;
> and thy word was unto me the joy and rejoicing of mine heart:
> for I am called by thy name, O Lord God of hosts.
> — Jeremiah 15:16

Your brother and friend in Jesus Christ,

Rick Renner

Unless otherwise indicated, all scripture quotations are taken from the *King James Version* of the Bible.

Scripture quotations marked (*NIV*) are taken from the *Holy Bible, New International Version*®, *NIV*® Copyright ©1973, 1978, 1984, 2011 by Biblica, Inc.® Used by permission. All rights reserved worldwide.

Scripture quotations marked (*NKJV*) are taken from the *New King James Version*®. Copyright © 1982 by Thomas Nelson. Used by permission. All rights reserved.

Scripture quotations marked (*NLT*) are taken from the Holy Bible, *New Living Translation*, copyright © 1996, 2004, 2015 by Tyndale House Foundation. Used by permission of Tyndale House Publishers, Inc., Carol Stream, Illinois 60188. All rights reserved.

Scripture quotations marked (*TLB*) are taken from *The Living Bible* copyright © 1971. Used by permission of Tyndale House Publishers, Inc., Carol Stream, Illinois 60188. All rights reserved.

Partnering With Jesus and Working With God

Copyright © 2022 by Rick Renner
P.O. Box 702040
Tulsa, OK 74170

Published by Rick Renner Ministries
www.renner.org

ISBN 13: 978-1-6675-0019-5

eBook ISBN 13: 978-1-6675-0020-1

All rights reserved. No portion of this book may be reproduced or transmitted in any form or by any means — electronic, mechanical, photocopy, recording, scanning, or other — except for brief quotations in critical reviews or articles, without the prior written permission of the Publisher.

4. "saying" — λέγοντες (*legontes*): the tense indicates saying and saying
5. "King" — βασιλεύς (*basileus*): king; highest ruler; emperor
6. "troubled" — ταράσσω (*tarasso*): to be agitated, shaken up, or troubled; an emotional upheaval
7. "all" — πᾶσα (*pasa*): all; the whole; every single part; picture of totality
8. "young child" — παιδίον (*paidion*): not an infant (βρέφος, *brephos*), but a young child in training
9. "house" — οἶκος (*oikos*): a house; not the cave in Bethlehem, because by this time they were in Nazareth
10. "fell down" — πίπτω (*pipto*): fall down; collapse
11. "worshipped" — προσκυνέω (*proskuneo*): to worship with all necessary physical gestures of worship
12. "opened" — ἀνοίγω (*anoigo*): pictures a grand and magnificent presentation
13. "treasures" — θησαυρός (*thesauros*): plural, treasures; a storehouse; cargo filled with treasure
14. "presented" — προσφέρω (*prosphero*): to physically carry; to bear toward; to physically carry toward; these treasures had to be physically carried into the house
15. "gifts" — δῶρον (*doron*): plural, gifts, indicating many gifts
16. "gold" — χρυσός (*chrusos*): plural, meaning many gifts of pure gold; profound wealth

SYNOPSIS

The five lessons in this study on ***Partnering With Jesus and Working With God*** will focus on the following topics:

- A Decision To Partner With Jesus From the Very Beginning
- A Decision by a Small Boy To Partner With Jesus
- A Decision To Partner With Jesus That Brought Dramatic Results
- A Decision by Women To Partner With Jesus' Ministry
- A Decision To Partner With Jesus to the End

The emphasis of this lesson:

The Magi — or wise men — were extremely influential and highly esteemed in the ancient world. As "king-makers," they had the power to enthrone or dethrone a king. They recognized Jesus as the King of all kings and partnered with Him by lavishly showering Him with a storehouse of opulent gifts and rare treasures.

Did you know that God calls you a "co-worker" with Him? It's true. In Second Corinthians 6:1, the apostle Paul declares that we are "…workers together with him…." The words "workers together" would better be translated as "co-workers," and it is taken from the Greek word *sunergos*, which is a compound of the words *sun* and *ergon*. The word *sun* is a preposition that connects one to another; hence, it carries the idea of *partnership*. And the word *ergon* depicts *work* or *a task*. When these words are compounded, it describes *two or more who are joined together in a common job or task*. We are co-workers with God!

The Bible is filled with one example after another of people who joined together with God to accomplish amazing things. In this lesson, we will focus on a group of individuals who entered into partnership with Jesus from the very beginning of His life. We know them as the wise men, and, as we will see, their proclamation of Jesus as "king" carried a much greater impact than most people have imagined.

Who Were the 'Wise Men' From the East?

The story of the wise men is recorded in Matthew's gospel, and it begins by saying, "Now when Jesus was born in Bethlehem of Judaea in the days of Herod the king, behold, there came wise men from the east to Jerusalem" (Matthew 2:1).

The word "behold" in this verse is a translation of the Greek word *idou*, a term used frequently throughout the New Testament, which carries the idea of *bewilderment, shock, amazement, and wonder*. As Matthew was recalling and recording the birth of Jesus years after the event took place, he was still filled with *wonder* and *amazement* over what happened. It is as if he was saying, "Wow! Can you imagine it? I am still astonished about the wise men that came to Jerusalem…."

In Greek, the words "wise men" are from the word *magos* — the plural form of *magi*. It describes *a group of priests and astronomers that were strongly influenced by Daniel* who served in Babylon many centuries earlier. When Daniel was taken to Babylon in about 600 BC, many scholars believe he became the head of the Magi, and as such his prophecies and writings were not only well-known but also considered sacred by the Magi for hundreds of years. Daniel possessed such a godly influence that the eastern Magi revered his faith, his prophecies, and the Scriptures he treasured. As a result, they believed — and were waiting — for a world leader to be born that Daniel had prophesied about. Actually, at the time of Jesus' birth there was a general belief among most religious leaders that a mighty world leader was about to be born, and that belief was due primarily to the writings of Daniel and other prophecies he had shared.

To be clear, these wise men — or Magi — were not three lowly kings or lowly priests traveling alone through the wilderness on camels. They were a group of very powerful men from the Median Empire looking for Jesus. They held a very authoritative position during that era and were, in fact, considered to be *king-makers*. With one word, these men could install a king or dethrone a king. The status they held was a blend of politician, religious priest, and scientist, making them the most powerful men in the East. We have no one in the world today to compare to the Magi.

The fact is, no one could be king in the eastern world without the endorsement of the Magi. Thus, kings were respectful — and even terrified — of the Magi. History reveals that once the Magi came to Rome to see Nero, and their arrival terrified him because he knew the power and influence they possessed. Nero rolled out the red carpet for the Magi and treated them like royalty. Ironically, this was the same ruthless Nero who was afraid of no one and killed anyone he wished.

Why Did the Magi Travel to Jerusalem?

At an earlier time — around year 39 BC — Magi from Persia had temporarily removed Herod from power. Remembering that situation caused Herod to become deeply troubled when they showed up again. The Bible says, "Now when Jesus was born in Bethlehem of Judaea in the days of Herod the king, behold, there came wise men from the east to Jerusalem, saying, Where is he that is born King of the Jews? for we have seen his star in the east, and are come to worship him" (Matthew 2:1,2).

Interestingly, the word "saying" is a translation of the Greek word *legontes*, and its tense here indicates *ongoing activity*. It means as the wise men entered Jerusalem, they kept *saying and saying and saying*, "Where is He that is born King of the Jews?" The word "King" is the Greek word *basileus*, which describes *a king, an emperor*, or *the highest ruler*. In this case, it is capitalized in the Greek just as it is in English, which denotes it is *the greatest and highest King to ever be born.*

The Magi were looking for the Messiah-King whose coming Daniel had foretold. They had waited and waited and waited for His arrival, and when the spectacular star appeared to announce His birth, they searched for this King of kings and Emperor of emperors so that they could worship Him.

How Many Wise Men Visited Jesus?

Now you may be wondering, *Just how many Magi came to see Jesus? Was it three? Or were there more?* Although some early Christian writers say there were three wise men that went by the names of Gaspar, Melchior, and Balthasar, others believe there were twelve, and while these details are unclear, there are some things we do know about the Magi. For instance, the magi priesthood that existed at the time of Jesus' birth was from "the east," so it's likely that these Magi came from *Babylon.*

We also know that when the Magi traveled, they did so in huge caravans. They were a group of highly influential and exceedingly rich "kingmakers" accompanied by hundreds — and perhaps even thousands — of people to assist them on their journey. In addition to military body guards, there were also many servants in the caravan who helped carry the needed supplies, the cargo, as well as the treasures the Magi were bringing to the King. When this huge entourage arrived in Jerusalem, it was quite a spectacle.

Now contrary to what we see on traditional Christmas cards, the Magi didn't actually arrive at the time of Jesus' birth. Instead, they showed up about two years later and visited Him as a toddler. The reason it took them two years is because they understood who they were coming to see. Jesus was (and is) a high-level king that deserved to be honored appropriately. Hence, they took time gathering gifts and treasures they were going to bring to Jesus — the one Daniel prophesied about, who would be the greatest King of all kings and Ruler of rulers ever born.

Why Was Herod Troubled?

The Bible says, "When Herod the king had heard these things, he was troubled, and all Jerusalem with him" (Matthew 2:3). The word "troubled" is the Greek word *tarasso*, and it means *to be agitated, shaken up, or troubled.*

It can also describe *an emotional upheaval*, which is exactly what Herod experienced at the news of Jesus' arrival.

Likewise, the Scripture says "all Jerusalem with him" was troubled. The word "all" here is the Greek word *pasa*, and it means *all*; *the whole*; or *every single part*. It is *the picture of totality*. In other words, *all of Jerusalem — every single part* of the entire city — was deeply disturbed, restless, and shaken up by the news of the birth of the King of the Jews. And the reason everyone was upset is because they knew from past experience that every time news of this nature came, King Herod went on a killing spree.

It is documented that He killed one of his own wives because he thought she was conspiring to take his throne. Similarly, he executed his brother-in-law for the same reason, and on another occasion, he murdered three of his sons after hearing rumors that they were planning to take his throne by force. So when all of Jerusalem heard the wise men say, "Where is he that is born King of the Jews?" they were thrown into an emotional upheaval.

Jesus Was a Toddler in Nazareth When the Magi Visited Him

After vigorously interrogating the chief priests and scribes regarding how, when, and where the "Christ" was to be born, the Bible says, "And he [Herod] sent them to Bethlehem, and said, Go and search diligently for the young child; and when ye have found him, bring me word again, that I may come and worship him also" (Matthew 2:8).

It's interesting to note that Herod called Jesus a *young child* and not a baby. In Greek, the phrase "young child" is *paidion*, which describes *not an infant*, but *a young child in training*. This is very different than Luke 2:12 where Jesus is called a "babe" — the Greek word *brephos* — which describes *a newborn infant only a few hours old*. The word *paidion* — translated here as "young child" — depicts a toddler that is learning to walk and talk and is likely no longer breastfeeding.

Although Herod had sent the Magi to Bethlehem, that is not where they went. Scripture tells us, "When they had heard the king, they departed; and, lo, the star, which they saw in the east, went before them, till it came and stood over where the young child was. When they saw the star, they rejoiced with exceeding great joy" (Matthew 2:9,10). Once again, we see the phrase "young child," which is the Greek word *paidion*, meaning *a young child in training*. Remember, the Magi had first seen the star announcing Jesus' birth about two years earlier, which meant they were looking for a young toddler, not a newborn baby.

When we read the story of Jesus' birth in Luke 2:1-20, it depicts His nativity in a cave that served as a barn for animals. But by the time the Magi arrived, two years had passed and He was no longer in Bethlehem with His mom and dad. Rather, He was living in Nazareth. This is confirmed in Luke 2:39, which says, "And when they [Mary and Joseph] had performed all things according to the law of the Lord, they returned into Galilee, to their own city *Nazareth*."

In the Presence of Jesus, the Magi Collapsed to the Ground

Matthew 2:11 tells us, "And when they [the wise men] were come into the house, they saw the young child with Mary his mother, and fell down, and worshipped him...." Notice Matthew uses the word "house," which is the Greek word *oikos*, the term for *a house*. Again, this was not the cave in Bethlehem where Jesus was born. It was a house in Nazareth. Once the 40 days of Mary's purification were completed and Jesus was dedicated to God, the Holy Family returned to their hometown in Nazareth.

When the wise men came into the house, they saw the "young child." Here again, we see the Greek word *paidon*, describing *a child in training*. Once more this confirms that Jesus was no longer an infant but a toddler. At the sight of Jesus, the Magi "fell down." This phrase is the Greek word *pipto*, which means *to fall down* or *to collapse*. Imagine the weight of the moment in which these wise men found themselves. After centuries of waiting for the fulfillment of Daniel's prophecies, the world leader they had been searching for suddenly became a reality right before their eyes!

Upon seeing Jesus, the strength of the Magi immediately drained from their bodies, and they collapsed to the ground in His presence. Prostrated before the King of kings, these highly revered dignitaries "worshipped" Him (*see* Matthew 2:11). This word "worshipped" is from the Greek word *proskuneo* — the same word used in Matthew 2:2 — which means *to kiss the ground when prostrating before a superior*. It is a picture of *worship with all necessary physical gestures of worship*. Worship was in the hearts and on the minds of these wise men. Their intention was to find the prophesied

King of all kings and bow themselves to the ground before Him in worship and adoration.

They Presented Jesus With a Storehouse of Treasures

Out of a heart of worship, the Bible says the Magi "…Opened their treasures, they presented unto him gifts; gold, and frankincense, and myrrh" (Matthew 2:11). The word "opened" is the Greek word *anoigo*, and it describes *a grand and magnificent opening*. This was not the opening of small gifts that are usually pictured on greeting cards as many have imagined. What they opened up and presented to Jesus was simply magnificent.

Specifically, Matthew says they opened their "treasures," which is the Greek word *thesauros*, meaning *a storehouse of treasures* or *cargo filled with treasure*. In this verse, the word "treasures" is plural, indicating there were *many treasures*. The word *thesauros* confirms that these were not three little gifts, but rather *large* and *numerous extravagant treasures*.

The Magi also "presented unto him [Jesus] gifts." The word "gifts" in Greek is *doron*, which is plural, indicating *many gifts*, and the word "presented" is the Greek word *prosphero*, and its use lets us know the size of the treasures the Magi brought. The word *prosphero* means *to physically carry*; *to bear toward*; or *to physically carry toward*. Thus, these treasures had to be physically carried into the house by the servants who were traveling with the Magi. They brought a storehouse of treasures and numerous "gifts" and gave them to the young Christ-child.

A Gift Fit for the King of Kings

Ancient records help us have an estimation of what the Magi gave Jesus. Traditionally, the size of diplomatic gifts given to a king was in proportion to the status of that king. Thus, if he was a low- level king, Magi would bring lesser gifts. If he was a high-level king, they would bring greater gifts of higher value.

Jesus was the greatest, most preeminent world leader ever to be born, and His coming had been prophesied for centuries. That said, the Magi would have brought enormous gifts that were fit for the highest status of nobility.

Anything less would have been viewed as a diplomatic snub for someone like Jesus who had the highest status imaginable.

Diplomatic gifts in the ancient world — the kind the Magi brought — would have included: vases, urns, plates, carpets, all kinds of clothing, and all kinds of items fashioned from gold, silver, and other rare and expensive materials. The catalog of gifts Jesus received would have been enormous, and their value would have been a literal fortune. The Magi were coming to the birth of the greatest leader in human history, and the gifts they brought would be commensurate with His status.

Matthew 2:11 tells us, "...They presented unto him gifts; gold, and frankincense, and myrrh." In Greek, the word "gold" is *chrusos*, which is plural, signifying *many gifts of pure gold*. This particular word for "gold" describes *the purest form of gold*. It was the same "gold" that dignitaries and kings used to make their cups, bowls, plates, saucers, platters, and many other articles. Furthermore, items made from *chrusos* — "gold" — were the kind that ambassadors or heads of state would have brought to another king. That is what they brought to Jesus — the King of all kings.

The value of these gifts of gold — along with the gifts of frankincense and myrrh — was off the charts. In keeping with the records of Eastern custom, a *low-level king* in those days who was visited by Magi would customarily receive 110 kilos of gold. By today's standards, that is more than five million dollars. Again, that was a gift for a *low level king*.

Jesus was not a low-level king, but the King of all kings! That means He was presented with gifts and treasures corresponding to His status. If the stars in the cosmos were announcing His birth — if they stood still to show where the King of kings was born — can you imagine the immensity of the gifts He was presented? The value was simply mind-boggling!

What Happened to the Magi?

Without question, the Magi brought their very best to Jesus. Out of generous hearts of worship, they partnered with Him from the beginning of His earthly existence, not even knowing He and His parents were about to flee to Egypt to escape the murderous pursuit of King Herod. Knowing Joseph would not be able to work, God miraculously supplied everything His Son would need through the extravagant gifts of the Magi.

Although the Bible records nothing about what happened to the biblical Magi after going back to their own country, we are provided with some information on them from early Christian writers. An early tradition claims the apostle Thomas met with the Magi on his way to India and declared the Gospel to them. After repenting and surrendering their lives to Jesus, Thomas baptized them into the faith. Because they had partnered with Jesus and were working with God to accomplish His plan, God blessed the Magi with the gift of salvation!

Friend, when you partner with Jesus and work with God to accomplish His purposes, you, too, can expect to be abundantly blessed!

STUDY QUESTIONS

> Study to shew thyself approved unto God, a workman that needeth not to be ashamed, rightly dividing the word of truth.
> — 2 Timothy 2:15

1. What new facts did you learn about the Magi (wise men) regarding their influence, their connection with the prophet Daniel, and the vital role they played in Jesus' life?
2. Of all the details presented about the explosive nature of King Herod, the Magi's visit, and the size and value of the treasures they gave to Jesus, what surprised you the most? Why?

PRACTICAL APPLICATION

> But be ye doers of the word, and not hearers only, deceiving your own selves.
> — James 1:22

1. The Magi were extremely wealthy and highly influential people whose words and actions carried great weight. Knowing their superior status and the fact that they searched for Jesus to *worship* Him, what does it say to you about their character? How does their example affect you in your worship of Jesus?
2. History tells us that the wise men traveled a great distance and expended a great deal of effort to locate Jesus. To what lengths are you willing to go to search out and experience the presence of the Lord?

(Consider what blind Bartimaeus did in Mark 10:46-52 as well as the efforts of the woman with an issue of blood in Mark 5:24-34.)
3. Once the Magi found Jesus, they lavishly showered Him with a storehouse of gifts and rare treasures. In what practical ways can you generously shower Jesus with your gifts?

LESSON 2

TOPIC
A Decision by a Small Boy To Partner With Jesus

SCRIPTURES
1. **2 Corinthians 6:1** — We then, as workers together with him.... [We are "co-workers" with God.]
2. **John 6:1-14** — After these things Jesus went over the sea of Galilee, which is the sea of Tiberias. And a great multitude followed him, because they saw his miracles which he did on them that were diseased. And Jesus went up into a mountain, and there he sat with his disciples. And the passover, a feast of the Jews, was nigh. When Jesus then lifted up his eyes, and saw a great company come unto him, he saith unto Philip, Whence shall we buy bread, that these may eat? And this he said to prove him: for he himself knew what he would do. Philip answered him, Two hundred pennyworth of bread is not sufficient for them, that every one of them may take a little. One of his disciples, Andrew, Simon Peter's brother, saith unto him, There is a lad here, which hath five barley loaves, and two small fishes: but what are they among so many? And Jesus said, Make the men sit down. Now there was much grass in the place. So the men sat down, in number about five thousand. And Jesus took the loaves; and when he had given thanks, he distributed to the disciples, and the disciples to them that were set down; and likewise of the fishes as much as they would. When they were filled, he said unto his disciples, Gather up the fragments that remain, that nothing be lost. Therefore they gathered them together, and filled twelve baskets with the fragments of the five barley loaves, which remained over and above unto them that had

eaten. Then those men, when they had seen the miracle that Jesus did, said, This is of a truth that prophet that should come into the world.

GREEK WORDS

1. "co-worker" — συνεργός (*sunergos*): compound of σύν (*sun*) and ἔργον (*ergon*); σύν (*sun*) is a preposition that connected one to another, hence, it carries the idea of partnership; the word ἔργον (*ergon*) depicts work or a task; compounded, two or more who are joined together in a common job or task
2. "great multitude" — πολὺς ὄχλος (*polus ochlos*): an enormous multitude; massive in size
3. "saw" — θεωρέω (*theoreo*): to watch act by act, like spectators watching a theatrical performance; same word for "theater"
4. "did" — ποιέω (*poieo*): to do; to make; to create; it is the same root for the word "poet"
5. "diseased" — ἀσθενέω (*astheneo*): a word that generally describes a person frail in health; pictures those who were feeble, fragile, faint, incapacitated, disabled; can also mean to be in financial need
6. "saw" — θεάομαι (*theaomai*): theater; to fully see; to contemplate; to fully see in full detail; to behold
7. "great company" — πολὺς ὄχλος (*polus ochlos*): massive multitude; an enormous mob of people
8. "unto" — πρὸς (*pros*): toward; directly toward
9. "buy" — ἀγοράζω (*agoradzo*): to buy; the word for a market
10. "prove" — πειράζω (*peiradzo*): pictures a test designed to reveal a deficiency
11. "pennyworth" — δηνάριον (*denarion*): a small Roman coin that was approximately the value of one day's salary
12. "two hundred pennyworth" — the equivalent of 200 days of salary
13. "little" — βραχύς (*brachus*): little; pictures a small amount; a fragment
14. "lad" — παιδάριον (*paidarion*): a very young boy
15. "barley loaves" — ἄρτους κριθίνους (*artous krithinous*): a fragile and inferior bread; a barley cracker
16. "small fishes" — ὀψάριον (*opsarion*): a small fish about the size of a sardine or minnow, usually pickled or dried
17. "what" — τί (*ti*): what, referring to a small minuscule detail

18. "many" — τοσοῦτος (*tosoutos*): such a huge multitude
19. "men" — ἄνδρες (*andres*): men only, not including wives and children
20. "five thousand" — adding wives and children and others, possibly 40,000 or more
21. "given thanks" — εὐχαριστέω (*eucharisteo*): pictures a free-flowing thankfulness
22. "as much as they would" — ὅσον ἤθελον (*hoson ethelon*): how much, how great, how many, as great as, as much
23. "filled" — ἐμπίπλημι (*empiplemi*): filled; doubly filled; filled to the brim and could eat no more
24. "remain" — περισσεύω (*perisseuo*): something that is overflowing, out of measure, beyond proportion; far-stretched; something that is incomparable, unsurpassed, unequaled, and unrivaled by any person or thing

SYNOPSIS

In our first lesson, we learned about the Magi from the East and how they held tightly to Daniel's prophecies for centuries concerning the arrival of the Messiah who would be the greatest leader the world has ever known. When the fullness of time came and Christ was born, the Magi traveled a great distance to come and worship the King of all kings and Ruler of all rulers. Lavishly, they gave gifts and treasures to Jesus, and in doing so partnered with God to help bring about His plan of salvation for mankind.

Just as the Magi became *co-workers* with God, so are we (*see* 2 Corinthians 6:1). The word "co-worker" is the Greek word *sunergos*, a compound of the words *sun* and *ergon*. The word *sun* is *a preposition that connects us to one another*, hence, it carries the idea of *partnership*. The word *ergon* depicts *work* or *a task*. When these words are compounded to form *sunergos*, it depicts *two or more who are joined together in a common job or task*. In this verse, it is a picture of us in partnership with God, which is what He longs to do. In fact, His greatest works are accomplished when He is working in conjunction with His people.

The emphasis of this lesson:

Jesus will partner with anyone of any age — including a young boy with a small sack lunch. In faith, this child surrendered his five loaves and two fish to Jesus, and in doing so he partnered with Him and saw God

bring about a miracle that's still talked about today. When we partner with Jesus and give Him what's in our hands, supernatural things take place!

Massive Crowds Kept Following Jesus Because of the Miracles He Did

One of the greatest things about partnership with God is that there is no age restriction. Regardless of how old or young you are, you can work side-by-side with Him and do things you never thought were possible. The little boy who gave his lunch to Jesus is a perfect example. The Bible says, "After these things Jesus went over the sea of Galilee, which is the sea of Tiberias. And a great multitude followed him, because they saw his miracles which he did on them that were diseased" (John 6:1,2).

When John says a "great multitude" followed Jesus, he used the Greek words *polus ochlos*, which describes *an enormous multitude* that is *massive in size*. This was a crowd that kept getting larger and larger, and the tense of the verb here indicates they kept *following* and *following* and *following* Jesus. Why? It was because they "saw His miracles." The word "saw" in Greek is *theoreo*, and it means *to watch act by act, like spectators watching a theatrical performance*. It is the same word for "theater." When this growing multitude vividly saw the power of God erupting right in front of them, it was the greatest performance they had ever seen.

John said the people saw the miracles Jesus "did" and were amazed. This word "did" is the Greek word *poieo*, which means *to do*, *to make*, or *to create*. What's interesting is that it is the same root for the word "poet," which lets us know that Jesus had a creative flair to His healing ministry. That is, He created eyes where there were no eyes, arms where there were no arms, and feet where there were no feet.

Those who were "diseased" were being supernaturally restored to health. In Greek, the word "diseased" is *astheneo*, a word that generally describes *a person frail in health*. It pictures *those who were feeble, fragile, faint, incapacitated*, or *disabled* and can also indicate *someone in financial need*. Sickness and financial debt often go hand-in-hand. Jesus was supplying creative and supernatural solutions to unbearable situations like these.

As Jesus Watched the Multitude, He Tested the Faith of His Disciples

John continues his narration of what took place that day by saying, "And Jesus went up into a mountain, and there he sat with his disciples. And the passover, a feast of the Jews, was nigh" (John 6:3,4). Somehow Jesus and His disciples were able to pull away from the crowd and catch their breath. At that time they were near the city of Capernaum, and from their vantage point, they were able to look out and see the First Century roadway that ran up to Damascus and down to Egypt. It was this very road — the Via Maris, which means "the way of the sea" — that the Jews in northern Israel would take to travel to Jerusalem, and because the Passover feast was near, it was teeming with travelers making their way south to the temple.

The Bible says, "When Jesus then lifted up his eyes, and saw a great company come unto him, he saith unto Philip, Whence shall we buy bread, that these may eat?" (John 6:5). The word "saw" here is the Greek word *theaomai*, which means *to fully see in full detail*, *to contemplate*, or *to behold*. Like the word *theoreo*, it, too, describes *a theater*, which tells us that as Jesus looked out, He could see the full drama of the people's lives unfolding before Him.

Once more, the people are described as a "great company," and they were coming toward Him. Again, this is a translation of the Greek words *polus ochlos*, describing *a massive multitude* or *an enormous mob of people*. When the Bible says they were coming "unto" Jesus, it is the Greek word *pros*, meaning *directly toward* Him.

As this scene was playing out, Jesus turned to Philip and said, "…Whence shall we buy bread, that these may eat?" (John 6:5). The word "buy" here is the Greek word *agoradzo*, which means *to buy* and is also the word for *a market*. The use of this term is the equivalent of Jesus saying, "Is there a marketplace close by that we can buy these hungry folks some food?" Of course the answer to this question was no, seeing they were out in the middle of nowhere.

Why would Jesus ask Philip such a question? John 6:6 says, "And this he said to prove him: for he himself knew what he would do." Although Philip was clueless and helpless to change the situation, Jesus had full knowledge and full power regarding what was happening. He knew what

He was about to do, but He said this to "prove" Philip. This word "prove" is the Greek word *peiradzo*, which is *a test designed to reveal a deficiency*.

Although the disciples had seen with their own eyes many mighty miracles of Jesus — including the wonders of Him walking on water, turning water into wine, and casting out devils — what they had *not* seen up to this point was a miraculous multiplication of food. They had a *deficiency* in their understanding of Jesus in this area. You would think that in light of all they had seen, they would believe in faith that Jesus would come through just as He had done so many times previously, but they were struggling. This shows us that no matter how long we have walked with the Lord, we always have room for growth — *always*.

What Exactly Were the Five Barley Loaves and Two Small Fish?

What was the response to Jesus' question? "Philip answered him, Two hundred pennyworth of bread is not sufficient for them, that every one of them may take a little" (John 6:7). In Greek, the word "pennyworth" is *denarion*, which was *a small Roman coin that was approximately the value of one day's salary*. Hence, the phrase "two hundred pennyworth" equals 200 denarii or *200 days' worth of salary*. Basically, Philip said, "Even if we could gather 200 days of salary in this moment and buy bread, it wouldn't be enough for everyone to have a little." The word "little" is the Greek word *brachus*, which describes *something small, a fragment*. Two hundred denarii of bread wouldn't have given each person *a fragment* to eat.

The Bible says, "One of his disciples, Andrew, Simon Peter's brother, saith unto him, There is a lad here, which hath five barley loaves, and two small fishes: but what are they among so many?" (John 6:8,9). It's interesting to note that the word "lad" here is the Greek word *paidarion*, which is a form of the word *pais*, meaning *a little boy*. When it becomes *paidarion*, it describes *a very young boy*, possibly five or six years old. This little boy had brought his lunch which consisted of five barley loaves and two small fishes.

Now, the Greek term for "barley loaves" is *artous krithinous*, and it describes *a fragile and inferior bread* or *a barley cracker*. And the phrase "small fishes" is a translation of the Greek word *opsarion*, which describes *a small fish about the size of a sardine or minnow*, and it was usually pickled or dried. Thus, this little boy had five barley crackers and two minnows that his mom had probably tucked into one of his pockets to eat on the way to

Jerusalem. Think about it: a five- or six-year-old boy would have no need of five large loaves of bread and two regular-sized fish; it would be too much for him to eat.

As the disciples searched for a solution to the food shortage, Andrew stumbled across this little boy with five crackers and two sardines and promptly brought him to Jesus' attention. Doubting it could make a difference, Andrew added, "...But what are they among so many?" (John 6:9). The word "what" here is the little Greek word *ti*, which means *what* and refers to *a small minuscule detail*, and the word "many" is the Greek word *tosoutos*, which describes *a huge multitude*. In light of the massive crowd, the lad's lunch was like a drop in the bucket.

How Much Food Does It take To Feed Forty Thousand People?

Looking at His disciples, "...Jesus said, Make the men sit down. Now there was much grass in the place. So the men sat down, in number about five thousand" (John 6:10). Notice the word "men" in this verse. It is the Greek word *andres*, which describes *men only*, not including wives and children. If Jesus would have wanted to describe *all the people present*, He would have used the word *anthropos* — but He didn't. He used the word *andres*, referring to the *men only*. The use of this word is the equivalent of Jesus saying, "Have all the husbands — the heads of the households — sit down." The wives and children then joined in and sat down, which is what we see confirmed in the other gospels where this story is told.

John 6:10 says, "...So the men sat down, in number about five thousand." This tells us there were "five thousand" husbands or heads of households present. When we add in the wives and children of these men and possible others traveling with them, the number in attendance that day was likely 40,000 or more. Can you imagine the amount of food needed to feed 40,000-plus people? It was certainly humanly impossible to do such a thing with just five barley crackers and two sardines. But "...What is impossible with man is possible with God" (Luke 18:27 *NIV*).

Although the Bible doesn't tell us specifically how Jesus ended up with the five loaves and two fish, we can trust that no one took them from the boy by force. More than likely, the child was brought to Jesus who then asked, "May I please have your crackers and minnows?" Rather than say, "No, You can't have them," the little boy surrendered what he had in his hands to

Jesus, and by doing so he worked with God and saw Jesus bring about a miracle that is still talked about today!

Thankfulness and Worship Open the Door for God To Work Wonders

Scripture says, "And Jesus took the loaves; and when he had given thanks, he distributed to the disciples, and the disciples to them that were set down; and likewise of the fishes as much as they would" (John 6:11). Standing in front of His disciples and the little boy who willingly gave up his lunch, Jesus "gave thanks." This phrase is a translation of the Greek word *eucharisteo*, which pictures *a free-flowing thankfulness*. Jesus' heart was so filled with gratitude that thanksgiving freely flowed forth. Instead of focusing on the miniscule amount of food in His hands, He looked to the Father and began to worship Him for His goodness. As He did, the food in His hands supernaturally multiplied.

John documents that everyone ate "…as much as they would" (John 6:11), which means every person ate *as much as they wanted*. By the time the meal was over, no one was hungry. In fact, verse 12 says, "…They were filled…." The word "filled" in Greek is *empiplemi*, which means *filled*, *doubly filled*, or *filled to the brim and could eat no more*. Thus, the people were feeling much like you feel after a Thanksgiving or Christmas feast — stuffed to the rafters. It was at that point Jesus told His disciples, "…Gather up the fragments that remain, that nothing be lost" (John 6:12).

How much did the disciples pick up? The Bible says, "Therefore they gathered them together, and filled twelve baskets with the fragments of the five barley loaves, which remained over and above unto them that had eaten" (John 6:13). Notice the word "remain." In Greek, it is the word *perisseuo*, which describes *something that is overflowing, out of measure, beyond proportion*, or *far-stretched*. It depicts *something that is incomparable, unsurpassed, unequaled*, and *unrivaled by any person or thing*. The use of this word lets us know that after everyone had eaten, there were remnants of crackers and sardines everywhere.

Scripture goes on to say, "Then those men, when they had seen the miracle that Jesus did, said, This is of a truth that prophet that should come into the world" (John 6:14). No doubt, the disciples were blown away by the multiplication of the food, and although the Bible doesn't say how the little boy responded to Jesus' miracle, he must have been powerfully impacted by what he witnessed. In faith, he chose to partner with Jesus, giving Him his five crackers and two sardines. Then he stood and watched as God worked through Jesus, taking the little he had and transforming it into way more than what was needed.

Friend, when you partner with Jesus and give Him what's in your hands, supernatural things take place. God blesses what we give Him and causes it to increase beyond our imagination. Are you ready to partner with Jesus and work with God in these last-of-the-last days? They are ready to partner and work with you, bringing dramatic results into your life and the lives of others.

STUDY QUESTIONS

> Study to shew thyself approved unto God, a workman that needeth not to be ashamed, rightly dividing the word of truth.
> — 2 Timothy 2:15

1. What is Jesus asking you to put in His hand right now? How is He asking you to partner with Him and work with God? According to verses like Ephesians 3:20; Proverbs 21:30; Job 42:2; and Second Timothy 1:12, what type of results can you expect to see in your life?
2. As a co-worker with God, He doesn't want you to worry or be anxious about anything. He wants you to trust and rest in Him. Take a few moments to meditate on Luke 12:22-34 and Romans 8:31 and 32. What is the Holy Spirit speaking to you through these passages? (Also consider the proactive principles found in Proverbs 3:5,6 and Philippians 4:6,7.)

PRACTICAL APPLICATION

> But be ye doers of the word, and not hearers only, deceiving your own selves.
> —James 1:22

1. The disciples had seen Jesus do many mighty miracles — including the wonders of Him walking on water, turning water into wine, and casting out devils. What are some of the amazing things you have personally witnessed that you know only God could have done?

2. Prior to seeing the miraculous multiplication of food, the disciples had a *deficiency* in their understanding of Jesus in that area. Are you aware of any deficiencies in your understanding of Jesus' power? If so, what are they? Where do you need Him to demonstrate His ability to supernaturally come through for you?
3. It was certainly humanly impossible to feed nearly 40,000 people with just 5 barley crackers and 2 sardines. But "…What is impossible with man is possible with God" (Luke 18:27 *NIV*). What seemingly impossible thing (or things) do you need God to do in your life right now?
4. Imagine you were one of the disciples who was there the day Jesus gave thanks and multiplied the tiny snack-lunch to feed the multitude. How do you think you would have reacted at seeing such a miracle? What if you had been the little boy who partnered with Jesus? How do you think seeing that miracle would have impacted your faith in Him?

LESSON 3

TOPIC
A Decision To Partner With Jesus That Brought Dramatic Results

SCRIPTURES
1. **2 Corinthians 6:1** — We then, as workers together with him…. [We are "co-workers" with God.]
2. **Luke 5:1-11** — And it came to pass, that, as the people pressed upon him to hear the word of God, He stood by the lake of Gennesaret, and saw two ships standing by the lake: but the fishermen were gone out of them, and were washing their nets. And he entered into one of the ships, which was Simon's, and prayed him that he would thrust out a little from the land. And he sat down, and taught the people out of the ship. Now when he had left speaking, he said unto Simon, Launch out into the deep, and let down your nets for a draught. And Simon answering said unto him, Master, we have toiled all the night,

and have taken nothing: nevertheless at thy word I will let down the net. And when they had this done, they inclosed a great multitude of fishes: and their net brake. And they beckoned unto their partners, which were in the other ship, that they should come and help them. And they came, and filled both the ships, so that they began to sink. When Simon Peter saw it, he fell down at Jesus' knees, saying, Depart from me; for I am a sinful man, O Lord. For he was astonished, and all that were with him, at the draught of the fishes which they had taken: And so was also James, and John, the sons of Zebedee, which were partners with Simon. And Jesus said unto Simon, Fear not; from henceforth thou shalt catch men. And when they had brought their ships to land, they forsook all, and followed him.

GREEK WORDS

1. "co-worker" — συνεργός (*sunergos*): compound of σύν (*sun*) and ἔργον (*ergon*); σύν (*sun*) is a preposition that connected one to another, hence, it carries the idea of partnership; the word ἔργον (*ergon*) depicts work or a task; compounded, two or more who are joined together in a common job or task
2. "people" — ὄχλος (*ochlos*): a massive crowd; a mob; an enormous crowd of people.
3. "pressed" — ἐπίκειμαι (*epikeimai*): to pile on top of
4. "saw" — ὁράω (*horao*) — to observe; to take note
5. "entered into" — ἐμβὰς δὲ εἰς ἓν τῶν πλοίων (*embas de eis en ton ploion*): however, having stepped into one of the boats; permission was not requested
6. "prayed" — ἐρωτάω (*erotao*): a strong request; to fervently demand with the expectation of a positive answer
7. "thrust out a little" — ἐπαναγαγεῖν ὀλίγον (*epanagagein oligon*): a nautical term meaning to put out a little into the sea
8. "sat down" — καθίζω (*kathidzo*): tense means having sat down; having seated himself
9. "taught" — διδάσκω (*didasko*): a systematic form of authoritative teaching from *Scripture*
10. "people" — τοὺς ὄχλους (*tous oxlous*): the large crowds; mobs of people
11. "out of" — ἐκ (*ek*): out of, from

12. "launch out into" — ἐπανάγαγε εἰς (*epanagage eis*): a nautical term meaning to launch out into the sea, with the Greek word meaning into; to launch into
13. "deep" — βάθος (*bathos*): deep; deep water
14. "let down" — χαλάω (*chalao*): to let down to a lower place; to go deeper
15. "nets" — δίκτυα (*diktua*): plural form of "net"
16. "draught" — ἄγρα (*agra*): a huge haul
17. "Master" — Ἐπιστάτα (*Epistata*): a master; a commander; in this context, Jesus as Master and Lord
18. "toiled" — κοπιάω (*kopiao*): to work to the point of exhaustion
19. "nothing" — οὐδὲν (*ouden*): absolutely nothing at all
20. "nevertheless" — δὲ (*de*): nevertheless; categorically
21. "word" — ῥῆμα (*rhema*): a spoken word; "at Your spoken word of direction"
22. "let down" — χαλάω (*chalao*): loosen and let down
23. "net" — δίκτυον (*diktuon*): fishing net
24. "inclosed" — συγκλείω (*sunkleio*): they caught; they trapped
25. "great" — πολύς (*polus*): pictures a great number
26. "multitude" — πλῆθος (*plethos*): a great number; huge amount; fulness
27. "net" — δίκτυον (*diktuon*): fishing net
28. "brake" — διαρρήσσω (*diarresso*): the tense means the nets were bursting
29. "help" — συλλαμβάνω (*sullambano*): to physically help take in the haul
30. "filled" — πλήθω (*pletho*): to fill to the maximum; fill to capacity
31. "sink" — βυθίζω (*buthidzo*): to sink; pictures a desperate situation
32. "fell down" — προσπίπτω (*prospipto*): to fall toward
33. "saying" — λέγων (*legon*): saying repetitiously
34. "depart from" — ἐξέρχομαι (*exerchomai*): to make an exit; to go away
35. "sinful man" — ἁμαρτωλός (*hamartolos*): pictures a sinner; one who has missed the mark
36. "Lord" — Κύριε (*Kurie*): Lord; absolute master or lord
37. "astonished" — θάμβος (*thambos*): dumbfounded to the point of shutting down

38. "at" — ἐπὶ (*epi*): upon, hence, upon seeing or upon the moment
39. "draught" — ἄγρα (*agra*): a huge haul
40. "fear not" — Μὴ φοβοῦ (*Me phobou*): a prohibition, stop fearing
41. "catch" — ζωγρέω (*zogreo*): to be actively catching; to catch alive
42. "forsook" — ἀφίημι (*aphiemi*): to permanently release; to let go; to discharge and send away with no intention of ever retrieving again
43. "followed" — ἀκολουθέω (*akoloutheo*): to follow after someone or something in a very determined and purposeful manner

SYNOPSIS

Turning our attention to our anchor verse, Paul informs us that we are *co-workers* together with God (*see* 2 Corinthians 6:1). As we have seen, the word "co" in Greek is the word *sun*. This word *sun* is a preposition, which pictures connection to someone else. And the word "worker" is a translation of the Greek word *ergon*, which is the term for *a task*, *work*, or *an assignment*. This is not you doing something by yourself or someone else doing something for you. It's a picture of you working in conjunction with someone else. When we compound *sun* and *ergon* to form the Greek word *sunergos*, it depicts *two or more who are joined together in a common job or task*. In this case, it's us working together with God and God working with us in partnership.

The Bible is filled with documented stories of people from all walks of life working in partnership with God to accomplish extraordinary things. In our first lesson, we saw how the highly influential Magi partnered with Jesus in the very beginning of His life, worshiping and honoring Him with their caravan of extravagant gifts. Then in Lesson 2, we learned how a young boy partnered with Jesus by sharing his tiny lunch that became a feast that fed over 40,000 people.

Indeed, when we partner with Jesus and work with God, supernatural results follow, which is what we're going to see again in this lesson. When Peter surrendered the use of his boat to Christ, the catch of fish that resulted was so enormous it was almost uncontainable. More importantly, this miracle was so impactful it caused Peter and those who were with him to lay down their fishing career and totally surrender their lives to Jesus.

The emphasis of this lesson:

Peter partnered with Jesus by allowing Him to use his boat as a pulpit from which He could teach the Word. As a result of his obedience, he and his fishing partners witnessed a mind-boggling catch of fish. More importantly, Peter's partnership led to his salvation and his launch into apostolic ministry.

Jesus Turned Peter's Boat Into a Platform To Teach the Word

Shortly after delivering a man with an unclean spirit in the synagogue and healing Peter's mother-in-law of a lingering fever, Jesus began moving throughout the towns in Galilee preaching in the local synagogues. The Bible says, "And it came to pass, that, as the people pressed upon him to hear the word of God, he stood by the lake of Gennesaret, and saw two ships standing by the lake: but the fishermen were gone out of them, and were washing their nets" (Luke 5:1,2).

In verse 1, it says the "people pressed upon Him." The word "people" is the Greek word *ochlos*, and it describes *a massive crowd* or *a mob*. As we saw in our last lesson, from the moment Jesus' ministry began, the crowds grew larger and larger with each passing day. In fact, at this point they had become so massive that they "pressed upon Him." In Greek, the word "pressed" is *epikeimai*, which literally means *to pile on top of*. The people who had come to hear Jesus speak and receive His healing touch were literally *piling on top of Him* as He was trying to minister.

To deal with the situation, Jesus got creative. When Luke says He "saw two ships standing by the lake," the word "saw" is the Greek word *horao*, which means *to observe* or *to take note*. When Jesus took note of the boats by the lake, He saw them as an opportunity. Luke 5:3 says, "And he entered into one of the ships, which was Simon's...." The interesting thing about the words "entered into" is that in Greek it actually says, "However, having stepped into one of the boats...." In other words, Jesus didn't ask for permission; He just seized the opportunity and stepped into the boat. That available, empty vessel became a platform for His presence and a pulpit from which He could teach the Word. Jesus will use any vehicle or vessel available to Him to bring the Word of God to as many people as possible.

The Bible says Jesus turned to Peter "…and prayed him that he would thrust out a little from the land. And he sat down, and taught the people out of the ship" (Luke 5:3). The word "prayed" here is the Greek word *erotao*, which is *a strong request and a fervent demand with the expectation of a positive answer.* Jesus strongly requested Peter to "thrust out a little," expecting him to say yes. "Thrust out a little" is a nautical term meaning *to put out a little into the sea.* When Peter complied, Jesus "…sat down, and taught the people out of the ship" (Luke 5:3).

In Greek, the words "sat down" are a translation of *kathidzo*, and the tense means *having sat down* or *having seated himself.* As soon as Jesus had seated Himself in Peter's boat, He "taught the people." The word "taught" in Greek is *didasko*, which describes *a systematic form of authoritative teaching from Scripture*, and the word "people" in Greek literally means *large crowds* or *mobs of people.* Jesus was the Word made flesh (*see* John 1:14), and as the walking talking Bible, He began systematically teaching the Scriptures "out of" or *from* the boat. It was natural for Him to take the Word and make it come alive everywhere He went.

Jesus Told Peter To Launch Out Into the 'Deep'

The Bible goes on to say, "Now when he had left speaking, he said unto Simon, Launch out into the deep, and let down your nets for a draught" (Luke 5:4). The phrase "launch out into" is another nautical term, and it means *to launch out into the sea*, with the Greek word meaning *into.* Jesus urged Peter to *launch into* the "deep" — the Greek term *bathos*, meaning *deep, deep water.* At that moment, the boat was sitting in shallow waters, and in order to reel in the huge catch every fisherman dreams of, one has to push out into the deep. Likewise, in order to experience the big things God wants to do in our lives, we have to go deeper in Him.

Once Peter was out into deeper waters, he was to "…let down [his] nets for a draught" (Luke 5:4). The words "let down" is the Greek word *chalao*, which means *to let down to a lower place* or *to go deeper.* The Greek word for "nets" here is *diktua*, which is the plural form of "net." Jesus knew a massive harvest of fish was about to happen, which is why He told Peter to let down his *nets* — plural — to take it all in. The word "draught" here is the Greek word *agra*, and it depicts *a huge haul.*

Exhausted, Peter "...said unto him, Master, we have toiled all the night, and have taken nothing: nevertheless at thy word I will let down the net" (Luke 5:5). Clearly, Peter could have questioned Jesus' request. After all, he was a seasoned fisherman, and Jesus was just a carpenter. But rather than argue, he honored Jesus, addressing Him as "Master," which is the Greek word *Epistata*, meaning *a master* or *a commander*. It literally means *one who stands upon the spot* or *one who is in charge*. In that moment, Peter recognized Jesus as the One with absolute authority.

Of course, Peter did remind Jesus that they had "toiled all the night" and had caught "nothing." In Greek, the word "toiled" is *kopiao*, which means *to work to the point of exhaustion — mental, emotional, and physical exhaustion*. This was the equivalent of Peter saying, "Lord, we don't have any strength left. We've worked all night and given it our all and have caught nothing." Interestingly, the word "nothing" — the Greek word *ouden* — means *absolutely nothing at all*. After hours upon hours of casting their nets into the water, they didn't have a single fish to show for their efforts.

"Nevertheless," Peter added, "at thy word I will let down the net" (v. 5). In Greek, "nevertheless" is the word *de*, which always functions like an exclamation that emphatically and categorically accentuates a point. The word "word" is also important, as it is the Greek word *rhema*, which describes *a specific spoken word from God to us*. By using these words, it's as if Peter was saying, "Upon hearing your spoken word of direction, Master — the One on the spot and in charge — I will do what You've told me to do and let down the net."

The phrase "let down" is again the Greek word *chalao*, meaning *to loosen and let down*. Thus, the implication here is that the nets had already been gathered and completely folded up. Jesus wanted Peter and his team to unwrap their *nets* — plural — to take in the huge blessing God was about to unleash. Although Peter did obey Jesus' instruction, he only let down one net (*see* Luke 5:5).

When Peter Obeyed, He Experienced an Extraordinary Miracle

What happened as a result of Peter's obedience and willingness not to lean on his own natural understanding? Luke 5:6 says, "And when they had this done, they inclosed a great multitude of fishes: and their net brake." The word "inclosed" here (with the *King James Version* spelling) is the Greek word *sunkleio*, which means *they caught* or *they trapped* "a great multitude of fishes."

Notice that the words "great" and "multitude" are both in the same sentence. Usually, only one of these words is needed as their meanings are much the same. The word "great" is the Greek word *polus*, which pictures *a great or vast number*, and the word "multitude" is the Greek word *plethos*, which depicts *a great number, a huge amount*, or *fullness*. The fact that both of these words are used indicates the Holy Spirit is making the point that the amount of fish they caught was unbelievably huge. It was so enormous that the Scripture says "their net brake."

The word "brake" here is the Greek word *diarresso*, and the tense used means *the net was in the process of bursting* the very moment Peter and his men were trying to pull it in. They were catching more fish than one net was designed to hold, which is why the Bible says, "And they beckoned unto their partners, which were in the other ship, that they should come and help them. And they came, and filled both the ships, so that they began to sink" (Luke 5:7). The word "partners" describes *legitimate business partners*, which tells us that Peter had a major fishing enterprise.

When his partners arrived, they "helped" Peter, which means *they physically assisted in taking in the haul* of fish. Luke tells us they "…filled both the ships, so that they began to sink" (Luke 5:7). The word "filled" is the Greek word *pletho*, which means *to fill to the maximum* or *fill to capacity*, and the Greek word for "sink" is *buthidzo*, which means *to sink* and pictures *a desperate situation*.

Interestingly, the capacity of these ships was quite large. We know from historical records that each vessel on this body of water was 10 meters long and 3 meters wide, which is 32 feet long by 10 feet wide, and each boat could hold between 5 to 6 tons. Thus, if both these ships were filled to capacity and on the verge of sinking, Peter and his fishing partners hauled in *over 10 tons of fish*! This enormous, mind-boggling catch was the result of Peter choosing to partner with Jesus and allow Him to use his boat.

Peter's Decision To Repent and Follow Jesus Was the Miracle After the Miracle

Luke 5:8 says, "When Simon Peter saw it, he fell down at Jesus' knees, saying, Depart from me; for I am a sinful man, O Lord." Peter had seen many signs and wonders Jesus did, but when the Lord miraculously touched his business, he could no longer keep his composure. The Bible says he "fell down," which is the Greek word *prospipto*, a compound of the words *pros* and *pipto*. The word *pros* means *toward*, and *pipto* means *to fall*. When these words are combined, it depicts Peter *collapsing* at Jesus' knees.

As Peter hit the ground in front of Jesus, he was "…saying, Depart from me; for I am a sinful man, O Lord" (Luke 5:8). The Greek word for "saying" here is *legon*, which means *saying repetitiously*. In other words, Peter kept *saying* and *saying* and *saying*, "Depart from me, O Lord. I'm a sinful man. I'm not worthy to be in Your presence. Leave me, O Lord." The phrase "sinful man" is the Greek word *hamartolos*, and it pictures *a sinner, one who has missed the mark and made mistakes again and again*.

When Peter fell to his knees, he acknowledged Jesus as "Lord" of his life. The word "Lord" here is the Greek word *Kurie*, meaning *Lord, absolute master, or lord*. Although Peter had had several prior encounters with Christ where He had seen Him heal multitudes of people, including his mother-in-law, he had not repented of his sin and made Jesus the Lord of his life. It was in that moment, when he called Jesus "Lord," that he was saved. The Scripture says, "Everyone who calls on the name of the Lord will be saved" (Acts 2:21 *NLT*).

Luke 5:9 and 10 adds, "For he was astonished, and all that were with him, at the draught of the fishes which they had taken. And so was also James, and John, the sons of Zebedee, which were partners with Simon…." The word "astonished" is the Greek word *thambos*, which means *dumbfounded to the point of shutting down*. The catch of fish was so massive that Peter and his partners didn't have the mental or emotional ability to process what had happened.

They were speechless "…at the draught of the fishes which they had taken" (Luke 5:9). The word "at" is the Greek word *epi*, meaning *upon*. Hence, *upon seeing this event* or *upon that moment* when they saw the "draught" or *huge haul* of fish, Peter and those with him were dumbfounded.

When Peter Partnered With Jesus, He Was Launched Into Apostolic Ministry

How did Jesus respond? Scripture says, "…And Jesus said unto Simon, Fear not; from henceforth thou shalt catch men" (Luke 5:10).

Peter was shaken to the core because he had never seen anything like what he had just experienced. When Jesus said, "Fear not," He used the Greek prohibition *Me phobou*, which means *stop fearing*. It is the equivalent of Jesus saying, "Put a halt to fear. Stop it and stop it now. From this point forward you will catch men." In Greek, the word "catch" is *zogreo*, which means *to be actively catching* or *to catch alive*.

Luke 5:11 tells us, "And when they had brought their ships to land, they forsook all, and followed him." The word "forsook" is a form of the Greek word *aphiemi*, which means *to permanently release*; *to let go*; or *to discharge and send away with no intention of ever retrieving again*. Thus, when Peter and his associates returned to the shore, they let go of their fishing enterprise and never intended to return to it. The miraculous catch of fish was a miracle that launched them into apostolic ministry.

In addition to permanently letting go of their fishing careers, the Bible says they "followed" Jesus. This word "followed" is the Greek word *akoloutheo*, and it means *to follow after someone or something in a very determined and purposeful manner*. When Peter, James, and John decided to follow Jesus, they really put their hearts into it and became the history makers we know of today.

STUDY QUESTIONS

> **Study to shew thyself approved unto God, a workman that needeth not to be ashamed, rightly dividing the word of truth.**
> **— 2 Timothy 2:15**

1. Even though Peter was exhausted from working all night and didn't feel like trying again, he stepped out on the *word* of Jesus and received a miracle in his business. In what area do you need a miracle? Is it in your *marriage*? Your *health*? Your *job*? Your *finances*?

2. Has God given you a specific *word of direction* or *word of promise* regarding the situation (or situations) you're facing? If so, what is it? What scriptures have the Holy Spirit made real to you?

3. If you need verses on which to stand and speak, use a Bible concordance and search by topic for what God's Word has to say on the subject. Write down the verses that energize you with hope and begin to speak them over your life, over your situation, and against the enemy.
4. One of the most powerful, life changing things you can begin to do is speak God's Word out of your mouth. Consider what God says in Hebrews 4:12; James 1:21; and Jeremiah 23:28,29. Ask the Holy Spirit to help you begin to speak God's Word faithfully.

PRACTICAL APPLICATION

> But be ye doers of the word, and not hearers only, deceiving your own selves.
> —James 1:22

1. The miraculous catch of nearly ten tons of fish left Peter speechless. Can you remember a time when the Holy Spirit showed up in a situation you were facing and His demonstrated power left *you* speechless? Take a moment and briefly describe what He did. How does remembering His faithfulness give you hope that He will come through again with what you're currently facing?
2. When Jesus saw Peter's empty, available boat, He stepped into it and began using it to reach others with the Good News. Today, He's still looking for available vessels that He can fill with His presence and use to bring life-changing truth to those in need. Are you available for God's use? What is God asking you to do right now to cooperate with Him and see lives saved and transformed?

LESSON 4

TOPIC
A Decision by Women To Partner With Jesus' Ministry

SCRIPTURES
1. **2 Corinthians 6:1** — We then, as workers together with him.... [We are "co-workers" with God.]
2. **Luke 8:2,3** — And certain women, which had been healed of evil spirits and infirmities, Mary called Magdalene, out of whom went seven devils, and Joanna the wife of Chuza Herod's steward, and Susanna, and many others, which ministered unto him of their substance.

GREEK WORDS
1. "co-worker" — συνεργός (*sunergos*): compound of σύν (*sun*) and ἔργον (*ergon*); σύν (*sun*) is a preposition that connected one to another, hence, it carries the idea of partnership; the word ἔργον (*ergon*) depicts work or a task; compounded, two or more who are joined together in a common job or task
2. "ministered" — διακονέω (*diakoneo*): from the Greek word *diakonos*, the Greek word for a servant whose primary responsibility is to serve food and wait on tables; picture a waiter or waitress who painstakingly attends to the needs, wishes, and desires of his or her client; these servants' supreme task was to professionally please clients; the servants served honorably, pleasurably, and in a fashion that made the people they waited on feel as if they were nobility
3. "substance" — ὑπάρχω (*huparcho*): goods, possessions, or property; only used to describe individuals of great wealth who possessed large fortunes or enormous assets
4. "healed" — θεραπεύω (*therapeuo*): therapy; carries the idea of repeated actions, such as a patient who visits a physician over and over until the desired cure is obtained
5. "infirmities" — ἀσθένει (*astheneia*): physical frailties, weaknesses, sicknesses, or a state of ill health

6. "out of whom went" — ἐξέρχομαι (*exerchomai*): a compound of the word ex, meaning out, as to make an exit, and the word *erchomai*, meaning to go; when compounded, it means to go out, to drive out, or even to escape
7. "devils" — δαιμόνιον (*daimonion*): evil spirits, demons, devils; the ancient world generally believed demons thickly populated the lower regions of the air and that spirits were the primary cause of disasters and suffering in the earth; this word could depict a person deemed insane; in both secular and New Testament writings, it depicted those possessed with evil spirits, who suffered with spirit-inflicted mental or physical infirmities
8. "steward" — ἐπίτροπος (*epitropos*): signifies a person who has been entrusted with the guardianship or supervision of another person's belongings
9. "many others" — ἕτεραι πολλαί (*heterai pollai*): very many and speaks of a great quantity

SYNOPSIS

Partnering with Jesus and working with God to see people saved, delivered, and healed is truly a privilege! Think about it: God is all-powerful and could certainly accomplish His plans on His own, yet He chooses to extend an invitation to each of us to partner with Him in the work He is doing in people's lives. The apostle Paul said we are "co-workers" with God (*see* 2 Corinthians 6:1), serving as His handpicked representatives to those who are lost.

This word "co-worker" is a compound of the Greek words *sun* and *ergon*. The word *sun* is a preposition that connects us to one another. Hence, it carries the idea of *partnership*. And the word *ergon* depicts *work* or *a task*. When these words are compounded, they form the word *sunergos*, which depicts *two or more who are joined together in a common job or task*.

- The Magi partnered with Jesus not long after His birth, providing Him and His parents with the resources they would need to live in Egypt as they hid from the murderous schemes of King Herod.
- The young boy with the snack-sized lunch partnered with Jesus, giving Him his five barley crackers and two sardines. Jesus miraculously multiplied the food and fed nearly 40,000 people who attended His meetings.

- Peter also partnered with Jesus, allowing Him to use his boat as a pulpit from which Jesus could teach the multitudes. As a result of his obedience, Peter and his fishing partners witnessed a miraculous catch of over ten tons of fish.

Friend, when you partner with Jesus and work with God, giving them what's in your hand to use as they see fit, the windows of Heaven open and supernatural blessings begin to flow into your life and the lives of those around you. God takes what we give Him, including our very lives, and "…[He] is able to do far more than we would ever dare to ask or even dream of — infinitely beyond our highest prayers, desires, thoughts, or hopes" (Ephesians 3:20 *TLB*).

The emphasis of this lesson:

Mary Magdalene, Joanna (the wife of Chuza who was Herod's steward), Susanna, and many others, partnered with Jesus by regularly giving of their finances and resources to support the spreading of Christ's life-giving ministry to others. They saw their partnership with Jesus as their supreme, God-given responsibility, and now they share in the reward of all the results reaped by His ministry.

God Noted in His Word of Certain Women Who 'Ministered' Unto Jesus

All through Scripture, we see that God is impartial and shows no favoritism (*see* Ephesians 6:9). Whoever accepts His invitation to partner with Him in His work, He will work with gladly. Young and old, married and single, male and female are all equal in His sight.

During Jesus' earthly ministry, there were certain women whose lives had been forever changed by Him, and as a result, they dedicated themselves to partner with Him and financially give into His ministry in order for others to experience the same kind of freedom they had experienced.

The Bible says, "And certain women, which had been healed of evil spirits and infirmities, Mary called Magdalene, out of whom went seven devils, and Joanna the wife of Chuza Herod's steward, and Susanna, and many others, which ministered unto him of their substance" (Luke 8:2,3).

Notice Luke said these women "ministered" unto Jesus. This word "ministered" is the Greek word *diakoneo*, from the word *diakonos*, which is very important. It described *a high-level servant* or *sophisticated and highly trained servants who served the needs of others*. The primary responsibility of these servants was to serve food and wait on tables. The word *diakonos* — translated here as "ministered" — is a picture of a waiter or waitress who painstakingly attends to the needs, wishes, and desires of his or her client. Their supreme task was to professionally please their clients in a way that was honorable, pleasurable, and done in a fashion that made the people being served feel as if they were nobility.

Without question, these women served Jesus with excellence. He had touched their lives and radically changed them, and out of extreme gratitude, they believed it was their God-given assignment to painstakingly attend to Jesus' needs, wishes, and desires. Their supreme task was to provide what He and His disciples needed to advance His ministry without hindrance.

Furthermore, the tense used in the original Greek indisputably reveals that these women did this task *consistently* and *regularly*. In other words, they habitually donated money to Jesus' ministry and became faithful partners on whom Jesus could rely. Serving the needs of Jesus with excellence and an attitude of gratitude is what we are all called to do.

They Gave Out of Their 'Substance'

How did these women give? Luke said "of their substance." The word "substance" is a translation of the Greek word *huparcho*, which describes *goods, possessions, or property*. This word would only be used to describe individuals of great wealth who possessed large fortunes or enormous assets. It lets us know that these were very wealthy women.

In the *King James Version*, it says these women ministered unto him *of* their substance, but in the original Greek, it actually says *out* of their substance. This implies that these wealthy women may have donated funds out of the income they earned on properties they owned or the investments they had made. It was out of their surplus that they sowed generously into Jesus' ministry. Again, they saw their partnership with Jesus and working with God as their supreme responsibility.

Jesus Had 'Healed' Them

What motivated these women to give into Jesus' ministry? The Bible says they "...had been healed of evil spirits and infirmities..." (Luke 8:2).

Notice the word "healed." Although there are several different Greek words that Luke could have chosen to use here, in this verse, he selected the Greek word *therapeuo*, which is the primary word used in the gospels to describe Jesus' healing ministry. It's where we get the word *therapy*, and it describes *a healing touch that requires corresponding actions*.

Interestingly, the word *therapeuo* — translated here as "healed" — carries the idea of *repeated actions*, such as a patient who visits a physician over and over until the desired cure is obtained. Just like a person goes through physical therapy and receives treatment again and again and again, the word *therapeuo* suggests that these women had been so severely demonized that although they were helped when they first came to Jesus, they had to keep coming back again and again until finally, they were completely freed.

It's important for you to understand that sometimes freedom comes to us in levels or degrees, and in order for you to experience a full healing and deliverance, it requires many touches of God's power upon your life. Just as Jesus literally *therapied* these women, He will therapy you as often as you come to Him. He will touch you again and again and again, as much as you need, until finally you are completely healed.

He Delivered Them From 'Infirmities'

Not only did Jesus heal these women of evil spirits, but also "infirmities" (*see* Luke 8:2). This word is a translation of the Greek word *astheneia*, which describes *physical frailties, weaknesses, sicknesses*, or *a state of ill health*. Keep in mind the word "healed" (*therapeuo*) is applied both to the women's deliverance from demonic spirits *and* to their freedom from illnesses. Therefore, just as the Greek suggests frequent visits were made to Jesus before they were finally and completely delivered from demon powers, it also implies that these women made recurring visits to Jesus before they found total relief from their physical maladies.

Again, the use of this word *therapeuo* lets us know, that it can sometimes take time before a physical healing is completely manifested in a person's life. It was through Jesus' compassionate touch and His willingness to repeatedly extend His healing hands that these women were set free from demons and restored to full health!

No wonder they were such avid financial partners with Jesus' ministry! It is simply a fact that the best partners in the world are those whose lives have been changed by one's ministry. These women are vivid examples of people with grateful hearts who want to do what they can financially so the ministry that helped them can reach out and touch others' lives as well.

Mary Magdalene Was Among the Women Who Partnered With Jesus

With precise historical accuracy, Luke begins to give recognizable names in this group of female supporters. The first is "Mary called Magdalene" (Luke 8:2). Now, Magdalene was *not* her last name. It actually refers to the town of Magdala — the place on the coast of the Sea of Galilee near Tiberias from where she came. People from Magdala were called *Magdalenes*. Hence, Mary was the woman from Magdala.

Over the centuries, many tales have been told about Mary Magdalene, but most of them have no basis in Scripture. For instance, you may have heard she worked in the prostitution business before she met Jesus. In 591 AD, Pope Gregory the Great inferred that she was a prostitute in one of his well-known messages leading up to Easter. However, there is no evidence of this claim in the Bible.

Unfortunately, this idea of Mary Magdalene being a prostitute caught on and was passed on for centuries. It wasn't until 1969 — nearly 1,400 years later — that the Catholic Church admitted the Bible doesn't support that interpretation. Actually, there isn't a single New Testament verse — or any other source — that says Mary Magdalene was a former prostitute.

The one thing we know for sure about this Mary is that she was possessed with an infestation of demons before Jesus delivered her. This fact is recorded in Mark 16:9, and Luke identifies her as "…Mary called Magdalene, out of whom went seven devils" (Luke 8:2). Notice the phrase "out of whom went." It is a translation of the Greek word *exerchomai*, which is a compound of the word *ex*, meaning *out*, as to *make an exit*; and the word *erchomai*, meaning *to go*. When these words are compounded, the word *exerchomai* means *to go out, to drive out*, or even *to expel or to escape*.

It appears that Jesus put persistent pressure on these stubborn demons, saying again and again, "Make an exit! Go out of her! Be expelled from her!" The "healing" He offered her was *therapeuo* — He repeatedly extended His healing touch until the desired cure was obtained. When these seven foul spirits finally made their exit out of her body, it is possible that they literally fled in order to escape the fierce pressure Jesus was exercising on them. Once they were gone, Mary was freed!

This brings us to the word "devils," which is the Greek word *daimonion*. It describes *evil spirits, demons,* or *devils*. In the ancient world, many believed demons (*daimonion*) were the primary cause of suffering and disasters. This word could also describe a person deemed insane. In both secular and New Testament writings, it depicted those possessed with evil spirits, who suffered spirit-inflicted mental or physical infirmities. This implies that when Jesus first met Mary, she may have had both mental and physical problems. But Jesus drove out all the evil spirits until she was totally free.

What's interesting is that the Bible has no concrete record of Mary's deliverance from these seven demons. However, it does let us know she was so thankful for what Jesus had done for her that she remained committed to Him to the very end of His ministry.

- She was present at Jesus' crucifixion (John 19:25).
- She was among those who prepared Jesus' body for burial after the crucifixion (Matthew 27:61; Mark 15:47; Luke 23:55).
- She was among the first to see the empty tomb (John 20:1), and she was the first to see Jesus after His resurrection (John 20:13-17).
- She was also the first to preach that Jesus had been resurrected from the dead (John 20:18).

Out of great gratitude for all Jesus did for her, Mary called Magdalene willingly used her money to financially support His ministry. She saw it as her God-given responsibility to partner with Jesus and work with God to finance the spreading of Christ's life-giving ministry to others.

Joanna, the Wife of Herod's Servant, Also Partnered With Jesus

As Luke continues to name the affluent women who financially supported Jesus' ministry, he tells us next of "…Joanna the wife of Chuza Herod's steward…" (Luke 8:3).

Notice Joanna's husband was a "steward." This is the Greek word *epitropos*, and it signifies *a person who has been entrusted with the guardianship or supervision of another person's belongings and wealth*. One of the rare appearances of this word in the Greek Old Testament Septuagint is where it is used to describe Joseph's oversight of Potiphar's household.

The use of the word *epitropos*, translated "steward," reveals that Chuza was no low-level servant. Rather, he was a high-level dignitary who served as the king's chief financial adviser and had the authority to make decisions on behalf of Herod in regard to his personal fortunes. The fact that Chuza held such a prominent position tells us that he was highly educated and was accustomed to managing massive sums of money.

No doubt, a man in this position had many opportunities to increase his own personal wealth as well, for he lived in the atmosphere of affluence and had many high-ranking political connections as Herod's steward. And it is safe to say that Chuza's resources were available to his wife, Joanna. Like Mary Magdalene, her life had also been dramatically touched and transformed by Jesus, which moved her to partner with Him and work with God.

Some scholars have speculated that Chuza may have been the nobleman talked about in John 4:46-53 whose son was miraculously healed by Jesus. If that is the case, it is easy to imagine how grateful Joanna would have been to Jesus for saving her child from death. Certainly a person so impacted would want to use her fortune to make sure others could receive the same touch of God.

Although the Bible doesn't tell us how Joanna made her first connection with Jesus, the encounter she had with Him apparently changed her life. From then on, she saw it as part of her responsibility to give of her personal substance to financially support Jesus' ministry. In fact, Joanna was also with Mary Magdalene and the other women who visited and discovered the empty tomb after Jesus' resurrection, which lets us know she was faithful to Him to the very end.

Susanna and Many Others Also Partnered With Jesus

After Luke specifically names Mary called Magdalene and Joanna the wife of Chuza, he includes a woman named *Susanna* (*see* Luke 8:3). This is the only reference to Susanna in the entire New Testament, and we know nothing more of her, except that she also ministered to Jesus "out of her substance." This implies that she was another wealthy woman who used her personal resources to partner with and support Jesus' ministry.

In addition to these three specific women who supported the ministry of Jesus, Luke notes there were "many others" who did the same. In Greek, the phrase "many others" is *heterai pollai*, which means *very many* and speaks of *a great quantity*. Amazingly, there were scores of individuals who supported Jesus faithfully with their personal finances. These were givers who considered it their responsibility, their service, and their assignment to make sure the needs of Jesus' growing ministry were financially supplied.

Although we rightly focus on Jesus and the great works He did while on earth, just think of the reward that is laid up in Heaven for Mary Magdalene, Joanna, Susanna, and the many others who gave of their substance so that all those life-changing meetings could take place!

These women are credited with countless healings, deliverances, and salvations that have taken place through the ages. Today they are experiencing rich rewards because they gave of their personal income to help advance the ministry of Jesus. They were His ministry partners, and in Heaven, they share in the rewards of the results reaped by Jesus' ministry.

Friend, if your life has been touched and changed by a specific ministry, it is right for you to desire to give to that ministry to show your gratefulness and to make sure others receive the same touch you received. So when God calls you to be a ministry partner, never forget that what you do is vitally important. The gifts you give from your personal income and assets can make an eternal difference in other people's lives.

It's true that your name may not be publicaly known, but don't let it bother you. Instead, rejoice that you're among the "many others" who gave to Jesus' ministry but were not mentioned by name. Rest assured your name is well known in Heaven. God sees all you have given to advance His Kingdom, and He will reward you abundantly for all your compassionate and faithful efforts.

STUDY QUESTIONS

> Study to shew thyself approved unto God, a workman that needeth not to be ashamed, rightly dividing the word of truth.
> — 2 Timothy 2:15

1. What new details did you discover about Mary Magdalene — including her life before coming to Jesus, her deliverance from demonic infestation, and her involvement in Jesus' ministry?
2. Mary Magdalene, Joanna, Susanna, and many others are credited with countless healings, deliverances, and salvations that have taken place as a result of supporting Jesus' ministry. What do these passages of Scripture say to you about investing your earthly resources now in order to reap an eternal reward?
   - 2 Corinthians 9:6-15
   - Matthew 6:19-21
   - Luke 12:29-34 (Matthew 19:21)
   - 1 Timothy 6:17-19

PRACTICAL APPLICATION

> But be ye doers of the word, and not hearers only, deceiving your own selves.
> —James 1:22

1. Mary Magdalene, Joanna, and Susanna, received both physical healing and deliverance from demonic spirits. In what ways has Jesus healed and delivered you? From what debilitating habits, hang-ups, or diseases has He set you free?
2. When the Bible says that Jesus "healed" these women, it uses the word *therapeuo*, which carries the idea of *repeated actions* and implies that *they kept coming back again and again* until they were completely healed and freed. What does this say to you about the healing and deliverance you are personally seeking God for?
3. The women Jesus healed and delivered demonstrated their thankfulness by financially giving and remaining committed to Him to the end of His ministry. How about you? How are you expressing your gratefulness to God for all He's done in your life? What would you like to do to show Him how much you love and appreciate His transforming work in your life?
4. Has your life been touched and changed by a specific ministry? If so, it's natural for you to want to give to them to show your gratefulness. What ministry do you feel God is calling you to give to — or become

a partner with — to ensure that others receive the same revelation of truth and divine touch you received?

LESSON 5

TOPIC

A Decision To Partner With Jesus to the End

SCRIPTURES

1. **2 Corinthians 6:1** — We then, as workers together with him.... [We are "co-workers" with God.]
2. **Matthew 6:21** — For where your treasure is, there will your heart be also.
3. **John 19:38-40** — And after this Joseph of Arimathaea, being a disciple of Jesus, but secretly for fear of the Jews, besought Pilate that he might take away the body of Jesus: and Pilate gave him leave. He came therefore, and took the body of Jesus. And there came also Nicodemus, which at the first came to Jesus by night, and brought a mixture of myrrh and aloes, about an hundred pound weight. Then took they the body of Jesus, and wound it in linen clothes with the spices, as the manner of the Jews is to bury.
4. **Mark 15:42-45** — And now when the even was come, because it was the preparation, that is, the day before the sabbath, Joseph of Arimathaea, an honorable counseller, which also waited for the kingdom of God, came, and went in boldly unto Pilate, and craved the body of Jesus. And Pilate marveled if he were already dead: and calling unto him the centurion, he asked him whether he had been any while dead. And when he knew it of the centurion, he gave the body to Joseph.
5. **John 3:1-3** — There was a man of the Pharisees, named Nicodemus, a ruler of the Jews: the same came to Jesus by night, and said unto him, Rabbi, we know that thou art a teacher come from God: for no man can do these miracles that thou doest, except God be with him. Jesus answered and said unto him, Verily, verily, I say unto thee, Except a man be born again, he cannot see the kingdom of God.

6. **John 2:23** — Now when he [Jesus] was in Jerusalem at the passover, in the feast day, many believed in his name, when they saw the miracles which he did.

GREEK WORDS

1. "co-worker" — συνεργός (*sunergos*): compound of σύν (*sun*) and ἔργον (*ergon*); σύν (*sun*) is a preposition that connected one to another, hence, it carries the idea of partnership; the word ἔργον (*ergon*) depicts work or a task; compounded, two or more who are joined together in a common job or task
2. "where" — ὅπου (*hopou*): exactly where; in the place
3. "treasure" — θησαυρός (*thsauros*): a treasure, a treasury, a treasure chamber; where one keeps money, riches, or investments
4. "there" — ἐκεῖ (*ekei*): there; exactly there
5. "honorable" — εὐσχήμων (*euschemon*): refers to people who have a good reputation, who have a good standing in society, or who are prominent, influential, and wealthy
6. "counselor" — βουλευτής (*bouleutes*): the word for a member of the Sanhedrin; same word used to describe Roman senators; because of this word, we know this position in the land of Israel was one of great honor and respect
7. "waited" — προσδέχομαι (*prosdechomai*): a hope or expectation; to fully and completely take something without reservation or hesitation
8. "craved" — αἰτέω (*aiteo*): to be adamant in requesting and demanding something
9. "Pharisee" — Φαρισαίος (*Pharisaios*): the separated ones
10. "ruler" — ἄρχων (*archon*): the chief one, ruler, or prince; to denote the rulers of local synagogues and members of the Sanhedrin who were the highest authorities in the land
11. "myrrh" — σμύρνα (*smurna*): an expensive yellowish-brown, sweet-smelling gum resin that was obtained from a tree and had a bitter taste; chiefly used as a chemical for embalming the dead; an extremely expensive commodity
12. "aloes" — ἀλόη (*aloe*): a sweet-smelling fragrance derived from the juice pressed from the leaves of a tree found in the Middle East; used to ceremonially cleanse, to purify, and to counteract the terrible smell

of the corpse as it decomposed; this substance was also very expensive and rare

13. "linen" — ὀθόνιον (*othonion*): a cloth made of very fine and extremely expensive materials that was fabricated primarily in Egypt

SYNOPSIS

One of the greatest motivations to partnering with Jesus and working with God is cultivating a heart of gratitude. When a person begins to truly understand just how much God and His Son Jesus have given and sacrificially invested into us, he or she can't help but give back! Gratefulness is what motivated Mary Magdalene, Joanna, Susanna, and many others to give abundantly and regularly of their finances to meet the needs of Jesus and support His ministry to others.

Along with gratefulness, having a genuine love for Jesus is a powerful force that moves us to partner with Him and work with God. It was this kind of energizing love that inspired Joseph of Arimathea and Nicodemus to give extravagantly to Jesus at the end of His earthly life. When these two men used their wealth to bury Jesus, they clearly illustrated their deep love and honor for Him to the fullest extent.

The emphasis of this lesson:

Joseph of Arimathea and Nicodemus were two members of the Sanhedrin who believed in Jesus and lavishly gave to Him at the time of His death. They were both highly respected, high-ranking Jewish leaders who used their prestigious position and great wealth to honor the Lord with an extravagant burial fit for royalty. Their actions demonstrate their deep love.

A Final Review of Our Anchor Verse

According to Second Corinthians 6:1, we are "co-workers" with God. This word "co-workers" is a combination of two Greek words: the word *sun*, translated as the prefix "co," and a form of the word *ergon*, which is translated as "workers." The word *sun* is a preposition that connects one to another; hence, it carries the idea of *partnership*. Moreover, the word *ergon* depicts *work, a task*, or *an assignment*. When these words are compounded to form *sunergos*, in describes *two or more who are joined together in a common job or task*. Specifically, it pictures you and God working together.

That is what we've been studying in each of these lessons.

- The Magi partnered with Jesus by lavishly giving of their vast resources.
- The little boy with five crackers and two sardines partnered with Jesus by giving Him his lunch.
- Peter partnered with Jesus by granting the use of his boat so He could teach the Word.
- And Mary Magdalene, Joanna, Susanna, and many others gave of their substance so that countless others might experience the life-changing touch of Jesus just as they had.

Everyone who chooses to partner with Jesus and work with God to see souls saved and see His Kingdom established in people's lives will be rewarded. Even giving something as small as a cup of cool water on behalf of Jesus is seen and noted by the Father (*see* Matthew 10:42). Indeed, as the Bible says. "…For whatever a man sows, that he will also reap" (Galatians 6:7 *NKJV*).

Two High-Ranking Jewish Officials Also Partnered With Jesus

Even at the time of Jesus' crucifixion, people were moved to partner with Jesus and give whatever they could to support Him. Specifically, the Scripture reveals two men who lavishly gave to Jesus at the time of His death — Joseph of Arimathea and Nicodemus. The Bible says:

> **And after this Joseph of Arimathaea, being a disciple of Jesus, but secretly for fear of the Jews, besought Pilate that he might take away the body of Jesus: and Pilate gave him leave. He came therefore, and took the body of Jesus.**
>
> **And there came also Nicodemus, which at the first came to Jesus by night, and brought a mixture of myrrh and aloes, about an hundred pound weight.**
>
> **Then took they the body of Jesus, and wound it in linen clothes with the spices, as the manner of the Jews is to bury.**
> **—John 19:38-40**

Joseph of Arimathea was a prominent figure during Jesus' day. He was from a little town in Judea called Arimathea, and he is briefly mentioned in all four gospels in connection with Jesus' burial. For instance, Mark writes:

> And now when the even was come, because it was the preparation, that is, the day before the sabbath, Joseph of Arimathaea, an honorable counseller, which also waited for the kingdom of God, came, and went in boldly unto Pilate, and craved the body of Jesus.
> — Mark 15:42,43

Notice that John describes Joseph as "honorable." This is significant because it is the Greek word *euschemon*, which refers to *people who have a good reputation, who have a good standing in society*, or *who are prominent, influential, and wealthy*. John also said that Joseph was a "counselor," which is a translation of the Greek word *bouleutes*, the word for *a member of the Sanhedrin*. It is also the same word used to describe *Roman senators*. The use of this word lets us know with certainty that Joseph of Arimathea held a position of great honor and respect in the land of Israel.

John also tells us that Joseph "…waited for the kingdom of God…" (Mark 15:43). This word "waited" — the Greek word *prosdechomai* — describes *a hope or expectation*. It means *to fully and completely take something without reservation or hesitation*. To be clear, this doesn't refer to a do-nothing, "hang-around-and-see-what-happens" kind of waiting. Rather, it pictures a person sitting on the edge of his seat waiting for something to happen.

That's what Joseph was doing. He was fully engaged and earnestly looking for and anticipating the Kingdom of God to arrive. Inwardly, he was ready to take it, to fully receive it, and to embrace it without any reservation or hesitation. This explains why Joseph was attracted to the ministry of Jesus. Because of his longing to see the Kingdom of God, he ventured out beyond his close circle of religious friends to see Jesus of Nazareth. His life demonstrates how **spiritual hunger is always a prerequisite to receiving the Kingdom of God**.

No doubt Joseph's willingness to think "outside the circle" of how others in the Sanhedrin thought made him unique in the supreme council. Nevertheless, it appears that the other members of the council shut their eyes and tolerated him due to his prominent position and extreme wealth.

Mark tells us that when Christ died, Joseph of Arimathea "...went in boldly unto Pilate, and craved the body of Jesus" (Mark 15:43). In Greek, the word "craved" is *aiteo*, which means *to be adamant in requesting and demanding something*. Normally, no one would speak to Pilate in such a demanding way, but because of Joseph's good standing, his wealth, and his prestigious and influential position, he believed he had the ability to apply some pressure and request that he might remove the body of Jesus before the Sabbath began.

The Roman custom was to leave the body hanging on the cross until it rotted or until the vultures had picked away at it. Afterward, they discarded the corpse in the wilderness, where it was eaten by wild dogs. But the Jews held the human body in great honor because it was made in the image of God. Even those who were executed by the Jews were respected in the way they were handled after death. Thus, it wasn't permitted for a Jew's body to hang on a cross after sunset or to be left to rot or for the birds to devour.

How did Pilate respond to Joseph's request? The Bible says, "And Pilate marveled if he were already dead: and calling unto him the centurion, he asked him whether he had been any while dead. And when he knew it of the centurion, he gave the body to Joseph" (Mark 15:44,45). If anyone could verify if a person was dead, it would be a centurion. After all, they were professional killers. Once the centurion certified Jesus was indeed dead, Pilate gave Joseph the body.

Nicodemus reentered the scene at this point. We say "reentered" because he had connected with Jesus earlier in His ministry. The first time we read about Nicodemus is in John 3:1 and 2, which says:

> **There was a man of the Pharisees, named Nicodemus, a ruler of the Jews: the same came to Jesus by night, and said unto him, Rabbi, we know that thou art a teacher come from God: for no man can do these miracles that thou doest, except God be with him.**

From this passage, we can determine quite a bit about the character of Nicodemus and what he thought of Jesus. First of all, we see clearly that he was a "Pharisee," which means *the separated ones*. The Pharisees viewed themselves separated by God for His purposes. Thus, they were extremely committed — and even fanatical — in their service to God. During Jesus' time, the Pharisees were the most respected and esteemed religious leaders in Israel.

Additionally, John said that Nicodemus was also a "ruler of the Jews." The Greek word for "ruler" here is *archon*, which means *the chief one*, *ruler*, or *prince*. Specifically, it denotes the rulers of local synagogues and members of the Sanhedrin who were the highest authorities in the land. Due to this high-ranking position, Nicodemus, like Joseph of Arimathea, was prominent, influential, and wealthy.

Nicodemus' notoriety among the Jews in Jerusalem was the reason he visited Jesus at night. His fame most likely created a stir every time he passed through the city. Therefore, he wanted to avoid visiting Jesus by day, as it would draw attention to the fact that he was spending time with a teacher the Sanhedrin viewed to be a maverick and out of their control. Consequently, Nicodemus came to Jesus by night when his visit would not be observable.

Nicodemus addressed Jesus as "Rabbi" (*see* John 3:2). This reveals a great deal about the intense spiritual hunger Nicodemus possessed. The word "Rabbi" means *great*, but it was also used as a title of respect exclusively for those viewed to be great teachers of the Law. The Pharisees loved to be called "Rabbi," for they viewed themselves as the chief keepers of the Law. But for Nicodemus — a high-ranking Pharisee — to call Jesus "Rabbi" was quite remarkable. It meant that he viewed Jesus as a scholar of Scripture or an authoritative theologian of the Word of God.

The fact that Nicodemus called Jesus by this privileged title, given only to those who were viewed as the greatest theologians in Israel, tells us that he was very impressed with Jesus' knowledge of the Scriptures. This means that Nicodemus, like Joseph of Arimathea, was open-minded enough to receive from people who were "outside the circle" of what most religious people viewed as acceptable. In fact, it appears he himself likely visited Jesus' meetings that had just been conducted in the city of Jerusalem. The Bible says,

> Now when he [Jesus] was in Jerusalem at the passover, in the feast day, many believed in his name, when they saw the miracles which he did.
>
> — John 2:23

Think about it. In order for Nicodemus to tell Jesus, "…Rabbi, we know that thou art a teacher come from God: No man can do these miracles that thou doest, except God be with him" (John 3:2), he would have had to have been to one or more of His meetings. It seems that Nicodemus had come close enough to these supernatural gatherings to personally view the miracles. This must have been the occasion when he heard Jesus teach and deemed Him worthy of the title "Rabbi."

As a Pharisee, Nicodemus believed in the supernatural. He was so moved by the miracles and so convinced of their legitimacy that he wanted to personally meet Jesus and ask Him questions. It was during his candid conversation, which is recorded in John 3:1-21, that Jesus told Nicodemus, "…Verily, verily, I say unto thee, Except a man be born again, he cannot see the kingdom of God" (John 3:3). This famous quote from Christ and the conversation He had with Nicodemus has been read, quoted, and preached all over the world for 2,000 years.

The Preparation of Jesus' Body for Burial Was an Extraordinary Display of Intense Love

Returning to John 19:39, it says, "And there came also Nicodemus, which at the first came to Jesus by night, and brought a mixture of myrrh and aloes, about an hundred pound weight." At this point in the timeline, Joseph of Arimathea had already secured the body of Jesus from Pilate and was now making the final preparations for His burial. When Nicodemus arrived to help, he came with "…a mixture of *myrrh* and *aloes*, about an hundred pound weight" (John 19:39).

The significance of "myrrh." The word "myrrh" describes *an expensive yellowish-brown, sweet-smelling gum resin that was extracted from a tree*, and it had a bitter taste. It was chiefly used as a chemical for embalming the dead. If you remember, this was one of the opulent gifts brought to Jesus by the Magi when He was a toddler. It was an extremely expensive and rare commodity.

The importance of "aloes." The word "aloes" describes *a sweet-smelling fragrance derived from the juice pressed from the leaves of a tree* found in the Middle East. Aloes were used to ceremonially cleanse, to purify, and to counteract the terrible smell of a corpse as it decomposed. Like myrrh, this substance was also very expensive and rare.

The mixture was about 100 pounds. Although many will read right over this verse, there is something extremely important that you don't want to miss. The Bible says that the mixture of myrrh and aloes that Nicodemus brought was 100 pounds. The reason this is extraordinary is because normally when a Jew was buried, loved ones used *one* or *two* pounds of myrrh and aloes, which was all that was needed. Nicodemus brought *a hundred times more* than what was required in demonstration of immense love for Jesus.

John went on to say, "Then took they the body of Jesus, and wound it in linen clothes with the spices, as the manner of the Jews is to bury" (John 19:40). The key to understanding this verse is found in the word "linen." This particular word in Greek describes *a cloth made of very fine and extremely expensive materials that was fabricated primarily in Egypt*. After they carefully laid Jesus in a large linen sheet of fine weave, the specially prepared spices were then mingled between the folds of this high-priced garment in which His body was wrapped.

Could Joseph and Nicodemus have used something less expensive to wrap the body of Jesus? Could they have prepared His body with one or two pounds of spices? Yes they could. *But this was Jesus!* And these men did everything they possibly could to express their deep love and honor for Him. As far as they understood at that time, this was their last opportunity to show Jesus how much they loved Him, and they were going to take full advantage of it!

This is an amazing story of two men who dearly loved Jesus, and they didn't just say it with their words — they demonstrated it by the giving of their finances and resources. Although Joseph and Nicodemus lived in circumstances that made it difficult for them to publicly follow Jesus, they chose to follow Him to their fullest capability.

What Does Your Giving Reveal About You?

Jesus said, "For where your treasure is, there will your heart be also" (Matthew 6:21). The word "where" in Greek is *hopou*, which means *exactly where* or *in the place*, and the word "treasure" is the Greek word *thesauros*, which describes *a treasure, a treasury*, or *a treasure chamber*. Literally, it is *where one keeps money, riches, or investments*. Thus, Jesus said, "The exact place where you invest and keep your money and treasures, that is exactly where your heart will also be." If we give little or nothing to the Lord and the advancement of the Gospel, it reveals that He doesn't have our heart. What we do with our money and our resources tells the truth about what we really love.

The heart of Nicodemus and Joseph of Arimathea was totally dedicated to Jesus, which is why they used their treasure to purchase the exquisite Egyptian linen cloth and the abundant supply of myrrh and aloes. He was their highest priority, so they invested their assets in showing their love for Him. They literally sowed their money into the ground when they bathed Jesus in 100 pounds of those rare substances, wrapped Him in an expensive cloth, and then buried Him in a rich man's tomb.

According to the words of Jesus, what you do with your finances really does tell the truth about what you love the most. As Joseph of Arimathea and Nicodemus honored Jesus in death, let's commit to honor Him with everything we possess as we serve Him every day of our lives. *Right now, let's make the choice to upgrade our giving, our living, and every other way that we are privileged to serve Jesus! Remember, as you partner with Jesus and work with God, you position yourself to experience God's supernatural power in your life.*

STUDY QUESTIONS

> Study to shew thyself approved unto God, a workman that needeth not to be ashamed, rightly dividing the word of truth.
> — 2 Timothy 2:15

1. Prior to this lesson, what did you know about the lives of Joseph of Arimathea and Nicodemus? What new facts have you learned about them? In what ways were they similar in their position and personal devotion to Jesus?
2. Nicodemus and Joseph of Arimathea were open-minded and willing to receive from people who were "outside the circle" of what most religious people viewed as acceptable. Why is this mindset so important? How did this attitude affect these men's relationship with Jesus?
3. Giving of our *time*, our *talent*, and our *finances* in partnership with God is a practice He wants all of us to develop.
    - What sobering yet inspiring words did the apostle Paul say about giving in Galatians 6:7-10?

- What did Jesus Himself say in Luke 6:38 you can expect to happen when you give?
- What does God specifically promise in Malachi 3:10 and 11 will happen when you give your finances?

PRACTICAL APPLICATION

> But be ye doers of the word, and not hearers only,
> deceiving your own selves.
> —James 1:22

1. Spiritual hunger is always a prerequisite to receiving the Kingdom of God. Be honest — how hungry are you for God? How strong is your desire to be in His presence, to be in His Word, and to know Him intimately? If you're not hungry for Him, don't feel condemned. Simply pray and ask the Holy Spirit to create a growing appetite for Him and to show you the nonessential things you're "full" of that you can eliminate from your life.

2. The Bible says that Joseph of Arimathea "…waited for the kingdom of God…" (Mark 15:43), which pictures him sitting on the edge of his seat expecting with full anticipation for the manifestation of the presence of God. How about you? Would you say that you're ready and eagerly anticipating God to move in and through your life? Are you looking and longing for Christ's soon return? If not, ask the Holy Spirit to show you what needs to change in your life.

3. Jesus said, "For where your treasure is, there will your heart be also" (Matthew 6:21). What would Jesus say your finances reveal about how much you love Him? If people were to look at the way you spend your money, would they be able to see that Jesus is the *highest priority* in your life? Do you treat Him with honor and respect in the way you serve Him, or is He the last priority on your list?

Notes

CLAIM YOUR FREE RESOURCE!

As a way of introducing you further to the teaching ministry of Rick Renner, we would like to send you free of charge his teaching CD, "How To Receive a Miraculous Touch From God."

In His earthly ministry, Jesus commonly healed *all* who were sick of *all* their diseases. In this profound message, learn about the manifold dimensions of Christ's wisdom, goodness, power, and love toward all humanity who came to Him in faith with their needs.

☑ **YES, I want to receive Rick Renner's monthly teaching letter!**

Simply scan the QR code to claim this resource or go to:
renner.org/claim-your-free-offer

WITH US!

 renner.org   facebook.com/rickrenner

youtube.com/rennerministries   instagram.com/rickrrenner

www.ingramcontent.com/pod-product-compliance
Lightning Source LLC
Chambersburg PA
CBHW061257040426
42444CB00010B/2404